First Facts™

Community Helpers at Work

A Day in the Life of a
Zookeeper

by Nate LeBoutillier

Capstone
press
Mankato, Minnesota

First Facts is published by Capstone Press,
1710 Roe Crest Drive, North Mankato, Minnesota 56003.
www.capstonepress.com

Library of Congress Cataloging-in-Publication Data
LeBoutillier, Nate.
  A day in the life of a zookeeper / by Nate LeBoutillier.
  p. cm.—(First facts. Community helpers at work)
  Includes bibliographical references and index.
  Contents: How do zookeepers start their days?—What do zookeepers feed the animals?—Who
helps zookeepers?—What tools do zookeepers use?—Do zookeepers take breaks?—How do
zookeepers help the community?—How do zookeepers care for animals?—How do zookeepers
end their days?
  ISBN-13: 978-0-7368-2632-7 (hardcover)   ISBN-10: 0-7368-2632-7 (hardcover)
  ISBN-13: 978-0-7368-4678-3 (softcover pbk.)   ISBN-10: 0-7368-4678-6 (softcover pbk.)
  1. Zoo keepers—Juvenile literature. 2. Zoo keepers—Vocational guidance—Juvenile literature.
I. Title. II. Series.
QL50.5.L43 2005
636.088'9'023—dc22   2003028046

Editorial Credits
Amanda Doering, editor; Jennifer Bergstrom, series designer; Molly Nei, book designer;
  Eric Kudalis, product planning editor

Photo Credits
All photos by the San Diego Zoo

Artistic Effects
Photodisc/Siede Pries, 11 (hose); C Squared Studios, 12

Capstone Press thanks Don Winstel of the Columbus Zoo and Aquarium, Columbus, Ohio,
  for his assistance in reviewing this book.

Capstone Press thanks Nicki Boyd and the San Diego Zoo, San Diego, California, for their
  assistance in the photographing of this book.

022015
008752R

Table of Contents

How do zookeepers start their days? 4

What do zookeepers feed the animals? 6

Who helps zookeepers? 8

What tools do zookeepers use? 10

Do zookeepers take breaks? 12

How do zookeepers help the community? 15

How do zookeepers care for animals? 16

How do zookeepers end their days? 18

Amazing but True! 20
Equipment Photo Diagram 20
Glossary 22
Read More 23
Internet Sites 23
Index 24

How do zookeepers start their days?

Zookeepers start their days by checking the animals in the zoo. Zookeepers make sure the animals are safe in their zoo homes. Zookeeper Nicki checks on the porcupine. It is awake and hungry.

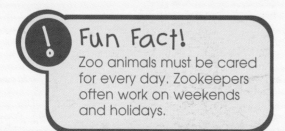

Fun Fact!
Zoo animals must be cared for every day. Zookeepers often work on weekends and holidays.

What do zookeepers feed the animals?

Zoo animals need the same foods they would eat in the wild. Nicki cuts fruits and vegetables for the monkeys.

Animals that are sick, weak, or **abandoned** sometimes have to be hand-fed. Nicki feeds milk to a young mole rat.

Who helps zookeepers?

Interns help zookeepers. Interns do many jobs at the zoo. Today, Richard sweeps out the petting zoo. Interns also help fill supplies and feed animals.

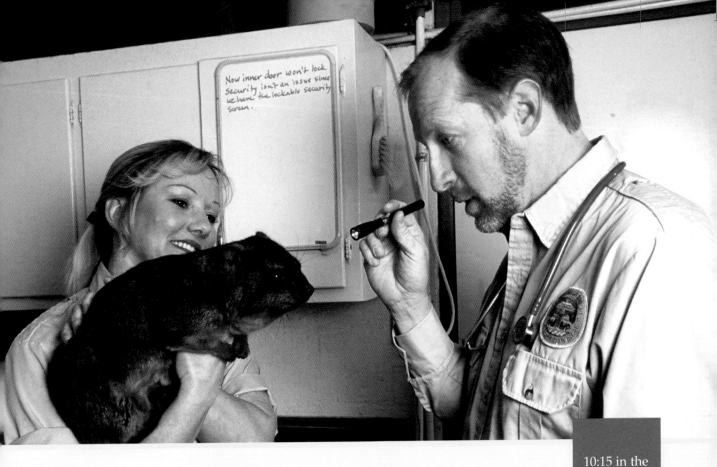

Veterinarians also help care for animals. They give animals medicine and treat injuries. Today, Dr. Young gives a checkup to a rock hyrax.

10:15 in the morning

9

What tools do zookeepers use?

Zookeepers use many tools. Nicki uses rakes, hoses, brushes, and shovels. She also carries a two-way radio to talk to other zookeepers.

Nicki uses tools to clean animal homes. She uses a hose to spray the otter home with water.

Do zookeepers take breaks?

Zookeepers take a break for lunch. A zookeeper stands or walks most of the day. Rest is important. Nicki often spends her lunch break in her office. After lunch, Nicki types **reports** about the animals. She sends the reports to other zookeepers.

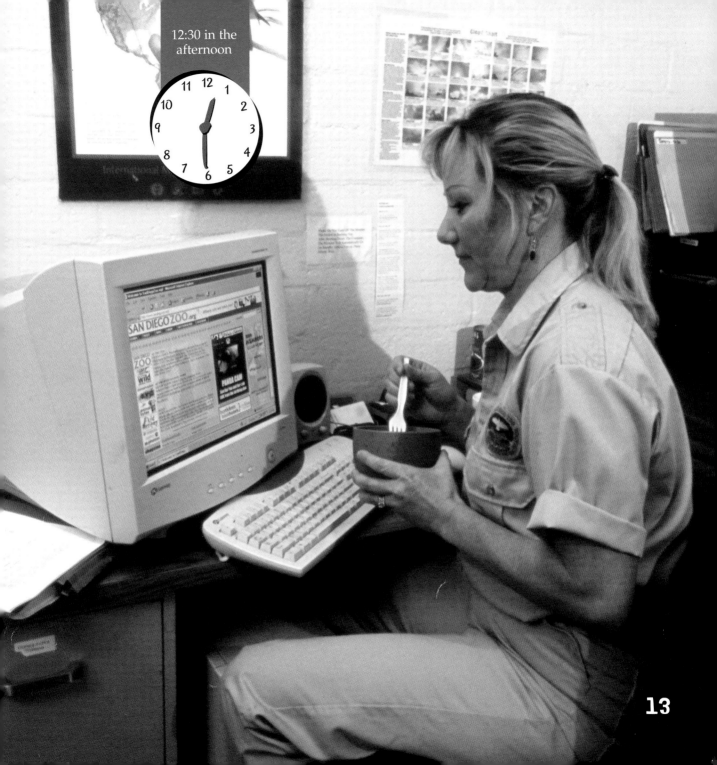

12:30 in the
afternoon

14

How do zookeepers help the community?

Zookeepers teach the **community** about animals. Zookeepers sometimes let people see the animals up close. Today, Nicki shows an owl to visitors. Many zoos have programs for kids. Kids can learn about becoming a zookeeper.

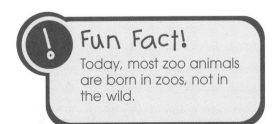

Fun Fact!
Today, most zoo animals are born in zoos, not in the wild.

How do zookeepers care for animals?

Zookeepers check the animals' homes. The animals' zoo **habitats** should be like their wild habitats.

Nicki spends time with the animals every day. She makes sure they are happy and healthy. Today, Nicki takes the Asian bearcat for a walk.

3:00 in the afternoon

How do zookeepers end their days?

Zookeepers end their days by checking the animals again. Nicki makes sure the red panda is safe and comfortable in its zoo home.

4:30 in the afternoon

Nicki greets the zookeepers coming in for the night. They talk about the animals. Nicki tells Melinda how she cared for the animals during the day.

Amazing but True!

Antivenin is a medicine made from the venom of poisonous snakes. Antivenin reverses the effects of snakebites. Antivenin can save the lives of zookeepers bitten by venomous snakes. All zoos that have venomous snakes must have antivenin.

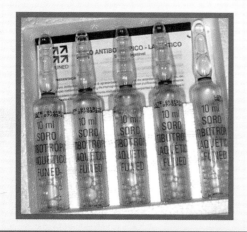

Stove

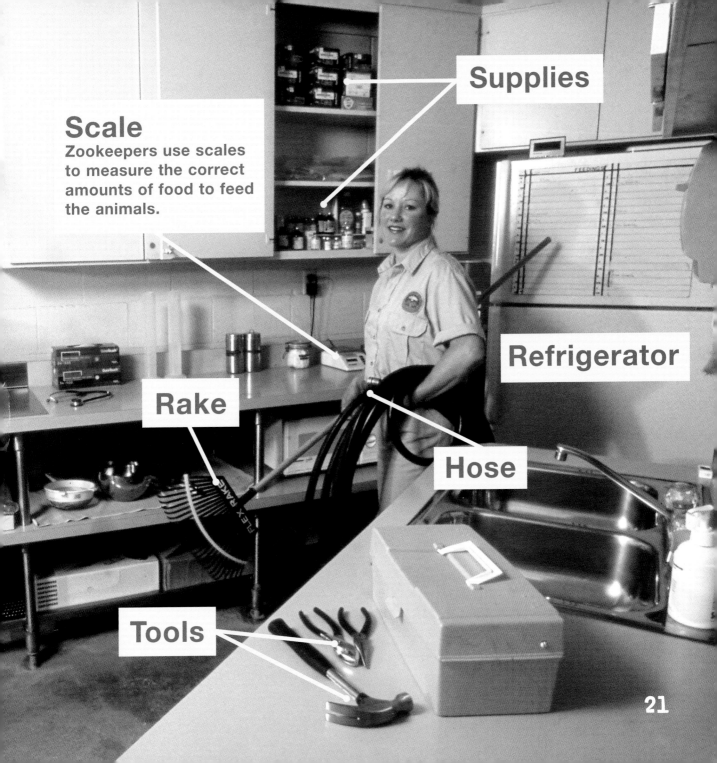

Supplies

Scale
Zookeepers use scales to measure the correct amounts of food to feed the animals.

Refrigerator

Rake

Hose

Tools

21

Glossary

abandoned (uh-BAN-duhnd)—left alone to take care of itself; some young animals are abandoned by their mothers.

community (kuh-MYOO-nuh-tee)—a group of people who live in the same area

habitat (HAB-uh-tat)—the place and natural conditions in which an animal lives

intern (IN-turn)—a person who is learning a skill or job by working with an expert in that field

report (ri-PORT)—a written account of something that has happened

veterinarian (vet-ur-uh-NER-ee-uhn)—a doctor who treats sick or injured animals

Read More

Liebman, Dan. *I Want to Be a Zookeeper.* Buffalo, NY: Firefly Books, 2003.

Miller, Heather. *Zookeeper.* This Is What I Want to Be. Chicago: Heinemann, 2003.

Internet Sites

FactHound offers a safe, fun way to find Internet sites related to this book. All of the sites on FactHound have been researched by our staff.

Here's how:
1. Visit *www.facthound.com*
2. Type in this special code **0736826327** for age-appropriate sites. Or enter a search word related to this book for a more general search.
3. Click on the **Fetch It** button.

FactHound will fetch the best sites for you!

Index

antivenin, 20

checkup, 9
community, 15

feeding, 6–7, 8
food, 6–7

habitats, 16
homes, 4, 11, 16, 18

injuries, 9
interns, 8

kids, 15

lunch, 12

medicine, 9, 20

programs, 15

reports, 12

supplies, 8

tools, 10–11

veterinarians, 9